Buddhist Esoteric Philosophy Of

Life

Hargrave Jennings

Kessinger Publishing's Rare Reprints

Thousands of Scarce and Hard-to-Find Books on These and other Subjects!

- Americana
- Ancient Mysteries
- Animals
- Anthropology
- Architecture
- Arts
- Astrology
- Bibliographies
- Biographies & Memoirs
- Body, Mind & Spirit
- Business & Investing
- Children & Young Adult
- Collectibles
- Comparative Religions
- Crafts & Hobbies
- Earth Sciences
- Education
- Ephemera
- Fiction
- Folklore
- Geography
- Health & Diet
- History
- Hobbies & Leisure
- Humor
- Illustrated Books
- Language & Culture
- Law
- Life Sciences
- Literature
- Medicine & Pharmacy
- Metaphysical
- Music
- Mystery & Crime
- Mythology
- Natural History
- Outdoor & Nature
- Philosophy
- Poetry
- Political Science
- Science
- Psychiatry & Psychology
- Reference
- Religion & Spiritualism
- Rhetoric
- Sacred Books
- Science Fiction
- Science & Technology
- Self-Help
- Social Sciences
- Symbolism
- Theatre & Drama
- Theology
- Travel & Explorations
- War & Military
- Women
- Yoga
- *Plus Much More!*

We kindly invite you to view our catalog list at:
http://www.kessinger.net

CHAPTER VI.

BUDDHISTIC PHILOSOPHY OF LIFE.

MATTER, in the sublime Buddhist view, is as the disease, efflux, refuse, or necessary means, method or glass, for the one unknown Rest, or nothingness, to be possible. Power is suicidal. Denies itself. Is not, nor can be, God. And power—which is alone God—implies the necessity of that power. Which necessity is superior to that power; which, in this view, and it is all that reason can give us, is alone God. God—like every other miracle—is possible only in intuition. Reason falls to pieces in our hands in our attempts to educe God out of it. For God is all. As well call the stroke the giver of the stroke, as God-manifested, God-Real. This is the Buddhist view, which demonstrated manifestation impossible: and therefore effaced power, movement, a God out of the universe:— meaning all things that can be, or the HUMAN REASON. But this is simply annihilating all REASON, or matter, and making SPIRIT the one universal only life—God of another kind. In Everything and the Only. Surely, a doctrine most sublime, and—as the last and ultimate—inspired.

Exertion presupposes the necessity for the exertion. Which is insufficiency. Movement is doubt. "One" and "two" are impossible. For the second is the conviction and consumer of the first. It is superior to it, and is the "first" worked out to itself, demonstrated or completed, else it could not be. It overrides and absorbs it, and is all it, in simply being:—proving the insufficiency of the "one." Power is disturbance;—which cannot be good. Out of the Nameless, from which comes Power, a third something is generated which is neither the first nor the second, but a sign; something accepted and different to either. But its "being" is its own "condemnation." And "being," or the "very possibility of being," is false in itself; though "necessary" for things to be possible. The first acts. The second is acted upon. And the third is the thing acted. The first is God. The second, in moving at all, contradicts the first as God, and effaces it. And the third is the Universe. Which alone remains. And this is untrue, and only a state, or condition, or mode, or bargain, or supposition, without any independent existence. Its laws are itself.

Now this is the Indian Trinity, as understood by the old Brahmin philosophers. And it is as equally Christian. For it lies deep buried in the foundations of metaphysics.

We underrate the great minds of antiquity in supposing that all of which man can think; all that to which nature is capable of replying, was not thought out, was not obtained in the far-past ages. Religions are not new. Belief is not new. God is not new.

When we look out upon the world, and survey—whether as developed in ourselves or apparent elsewhere—this extraordinary thing called BEING, the first idea that we obtain of it is, that the very thinking of it is contradictory and negative. That, in fact, the exertion of the mind is a thing against the purpose and design of the world. That we were born to be the " ideas," and not the " things thinking the ideas." That the phantom-world of shows was, in reality, THE world, and not the medium (or means) in which they were exhibited. This very fact, if believed—which it is never intended that it should be—would annihilate body, and make the visions of things, or picture-like ideas, the very things themselves. And not the *things*.

We have no business to think of thinking. We are the thing itself (in the short word) about which we strive to think. And the very first attempt to stretch attention into conception is force, and therefore unpleasant; is—and there can be no doubt about it—an effort in regard of the mental strength, greatly resembling the unnecessary strength of the arm (abstractedly speaking) put forth in the bending of a bow. That in our full health—*that in our perfect being—that in our man's completeness*, we are the mirror, or glass, of that outside (in its totality broken up, in the very necessity of the thing, into parts or particles, in order that, by succession or instalment, it may be received), is a foundation-truth, to which, however, we only become alive when we temporarily eject ourselves *out of ourselves* to see it. It is only in the infinitesimally small succession of ideas, or the admission of them, and in the passing through of them, one at a time, through this viaduct, or passage, or narrow channel, or *means* of the constructive human mind (that presses self, as it were, and makes ideas), that the great mass or bulk of the " exterior" intensifies inwards and concentrates itself, so to speak, into conceptive atoms. To pass through, and to become aware of (in a sort of deglutition), in the "intelligence." Ideas pass through the mind like sand-grains filtrating through the fine long hollow of a shell, or as the exquisite atoms of the invisibly minute air through a tube, and causing the whistling, admitting (however instantaneous the succession) one grain or atom alone—as one idea alone—at a time.

Compound ideas, admitted as compound ideas, are impossible. And the very idea escapes in our attempt to make it an idea. So reluctant and so evasive are notions, and so singular a machine is the human mind, that the effort to form an idea (of ourselves, and by our own motion towards it, and not as the mere accepting it or admission of it as presented from the outside) is painful. And the very act is accompanied by a contraction, or is produced as by a sort of convulsion. A man contracts his brows when he endeavours to recall anything far behind in the magazines of memory, or when he seems to direct his mind (from itself) upon any external matter not admitted as our impression of the panorama from without, in which he is altogether passive. And the thought of a thing is a mentally muscular operation, in which there is the same kind of action as bodily action. The purely natural state of a man, without his own exertion from himself, is entire unmotived unconsciousness. Permitting the outside to flow, as it were, through him; as if the arch of a bridge should become the stream as it flows through it, or as if the glass should be the images reflected in the glass.

Two things, unlike each other, cannot last. Two

things, in the metaphysic sense, cannot be. Because, if they were both produced at once, they must be independent of each other, and equal powers and antagonistic powers, else they could not be separate. If they are alike, they must blend. If they are separate, they must be repulsions. But it is impossible they can both be equal, and not form one. For there must be a ground of difference to make them "two," and that ground of difference must be on the one side or the other. On whichever side the ground of difference may be, that side must be the inferior, in the fact of there being difference, and not completeness, to itself. The very admission of difference implying inferiority to that which hath no difference. Power is perfect and whole. There cannot be two powers, for the second power is only the first power under another name. First is all, or it is nothing.

If we examine the materials of which the world, in the general sense, is composed, we find it made up of substance, and of something which governs and rules, and constitutes that substance, which is spirit. Spirit has no *substratum* by which to produce results to us men. It has no laws, no rules, no precedence, no "one going before the other," nothing to be known by, nothing to be appreciated by. It deals with abstract qualities. It has nothing which we can see or handle. It is only to be understood as something moving on, and making sensible, exterior things. Now, as a man is a machine, or compound of certain motive powers, or senses, produced out of the affections of the matter outside of him, there is necessitated to him a medium, groundwork, or floor or basis, on which his powers or gifts (in other words, on which he, himself,) shall have operation.

Mind and matter may be two worlds identical, or rather one and the same thing. Of the world of matter we have means of cognisance in our senses, which walk upon it, breathe it, see it, hear it—in short, are made up of it and make it. As things, in the sense, are agreeable or otherwise, do we seek them or otherwise. And we call them good, or not good, as they happen to agree, or to disagree, with the senses that approximate to them, or that are their objects, or that, in fact, are the senses.

But this, when admitted to the uttermost, will carry us no farther than to a certain coincidence, and a certain happiness, to the several senses. And we only obtain, not a truth of real good, or real evil, but only a relation to the life which we live, and which—out of us—we have no business to affirm, and to take for granted, as any farther life than *our* life. That is, relation.

All that can be got out of the world is the third thing called relation; the point of the triangle, being neither the left-hand corner, which is power; carried along the base line into the right-hand corner, which is that "empowered" or acted upon; and both acting and reacting, to and fro, along the lower level, and directed and swept up to result, or end, or identity of both—being that new third thing, and only true thing—relation: or the point.

Why deal we with *comparison*, when the life of the swine is the perfectest to the nature of that swine? When the fill of evil is the perfection of the evil.

When the life of the bad man is just that life which he, with an aim to excellence—that is, with the insisting of the perfect conforming of means to end, of patient and agent, of the squaring and regulating with the objects to be squared and regulated, of the working up of the sum set him (in his bad man's nature) to be worked up—should live.

Sin, or time, being the thing to be done, or shown, by his bad nature, or "clock-work," who shall blame a man for producing the very thing "set;" the only thing unavoidable? His nature being to make something of his nature, shall we quarrel with him, or say he is wrong, in producing this very result? We may as well blame the sword for cutting, when therein it discharges itself of its very duty. In short, we are here contending for the very faithfulness of nature, who does her own best true work in presenting THAT— and not that other thing—which her own constitution, in the very vitality and completeness of the thing, necessitates. We hold with the soundest philosophers, that nothing is imported into nature other than that which is to be found in it. That, self-complete to its circumference, nothing from the outside, is, or can be (from the nature of being), introduced from without. It knowing nothing, and having nothing, of that outside.

It is as if a man, asked to supply a means of measuring that which, in its own nature, is incapable of measurement, should offer his measure. It is as if an absurd person solicited, by means of colours, to produce a picture, should seek to paint, or make-out, or constitute his picture with the sums of arithmetic.

There is nothing surer than that two things, with no basis of likeness, cannot be both real. Matter and spirit have nothing in common. Therefore they cannot be both true. One must be unreal, and a deceit. And as, in the investigation into matter, the solids are lost out of the appreciative hands, it follows that there is no matter, and that the universe of things is all spirit. And that, as in the world of being we are not "spirit," and anything conceived must be in "being" or under form of some kind, therefore that all form, or being, is a show only, and unreal. All the real, *in its very necessity of-being real,* being empty of comparison (which makes being), and exempt of form and everything conceivable, and therefore (most logically and conclusively) nothing. Now, the sin or excess of "nothing," and its very denial and annihilation, is form, and the guiltiness of the "nothing-beyond-supposable" must be the "something-yet-supposable." And, therefore, "existence," or the "sense to itself," must be evil. Thus, demolishing matter, we superadd something better upon it.

Perfection is a relative term, having no connection with that thing which a man, in his self-deceit, calls good. Given an end—whatever machinery works towards that end; whatever means bring that end about:—what play of process realises that result, those means must be good, that end perfect. For the very idea of good, metaphysically, is only arbitrary vapour. The very notion of good, better, best; or bad, or worse, or worst, is a mere measure of comparison, or a spreading-out like any spreading-out, or opening-out, of completeness, perfection, or of nothing, to *make being.* We will illustrate our meaning by our example. A ray of light is white, colourless, objectless; is nothing. No eye-like machinery is set to decompose it, to untwine it out of its "oneness," to make comparison, or reality, or being out of it. It is nothing, has no existence, inasmuch as it has no laws, whereupon to set its *radii* of differences (like points of compasses), and circumvolve a world from out the start of them. How shall we attain to being (in other words, to reality of it), or of qualities, out of this non-entity? This non-existence is made by, and is, and is nothing *farther* than "laws" beyond which it cannot be conceived, nor can be anything. By force upon the thing, which must be *all* of the thing, since the mind can take in nothing farther of it, there shall be display, opening-out, analysis, "second out of first," divergence, comparison. And existence! Schopenhauser's thesis is cheerful: he says: *the existence of the world is sin*, and its essence *misery*. Then come "laws;" then come "things;" then come affections; then come attractions and repulsions; then come movement and passion: in short, to the apprehension, then come colours, or differences, or *other than nothing.* And between these worlds of affections of body (called colours or differences) lie man and all possibility. Nothing conceived, or conceivable, being other than it. Beyond these laws and necessities of being (in being) there lies nothing. It standing as the Eternal-Matterless, in which there lie no world of shows, in their vexatious undulations, and in their necessarily deceiving (for life to be) manners, to cause comparison. No realm of matter, in the ever-changing modifications of unity, or the "uniform," or the "nothing," through which (in the solid sense) to move the sensible, the ever-producing, and the ever-creating magnetism or Life.

The spiritual gulf of nothingness which (in the metaphysic, that is, in the humanly-reasonable, or false, idea) is, and can be, alone, God, it is impossible to conceive as mind or an underlying means, or, so to speak, as the floor of sensitive and lightening and cogent Power. Over which to go rolling the mind-forces in their ever-spreading, slackening, swelling or subsiding, individual, subsidiary and self-exerted appetence and strength. In short, outside of laws and necessary shows—exterior of the splendid, mo-tived, coloured, and sun-sense illuminated rings of life, in which deceived, and necessarily deceived, man is struck the centre (as the wondrous spark to find them fellow-fire, and false), lies nothing—or matter-less. Passionless Rest. To which Rest the Buddhist assures that all form, or seeming, or illusion, or pur-gatorial "swathes," or confines of cogence and life, or "being," in its amplitude of meaning, is tending. Controlling and centrifugatory from off the great cen-tral and immortal Light, where motion and com-parison, or good, or better, are unknown, but all is Rest and nothingness. This is the world of sense, or as in the waves of experience, or as in the pro-cession of the cycles, or as in the fields, and wreaking into show, of TRANSMIGRATION, like the multiform and ever-brightening, ever-blackening, ever-self-thinning, and ever-purifying, smokes. Birthing and carrying over their own nature, in the restless wheel, as greater

or as lesser, as grander or as baser, as the holier or
the worse, through time immemorial—made only time
in the measure of the changes—each and centrically
seeking, in return, to that SPLENDOUR of NOTHINGNESS,
from which issued, first, as expiation, and, as existing,
forms (to, therefore, expiate, of body), all things know-
able, and, therefore, all things bad—all " being," and,
therefore, all consciousness.

This is the great gulf of Nothingness, or of broad,
unmotived Spirit, or of immortal Fire, clear and vacant,
into which everything must he committed—everything
cast, of the conceivable, to be lost of itself. This—
as the great material element of Fire can swallow all
things, of the worlds, in its devouring jaws; searching
through, and taking in, their essences, into itself—
rather insinuating itself through, and disclosing its own
glorious countenance, through their far-sundered atoms,
till the very solid matter shall disappear; fire opening,
from the centre, out as the broader floor, down to
which, in our chemic, penetrating exploration, searching through the media of evolution, we have at last
awfully come! all nature being rendered up in its
fierce search, and in its not-to-be-contradicted (in the
world) forces and truly supernatural power.

Possibility collapses in the very idea of an addition
to unity. Since that which cannot exist of itself, and
needs something else to make itself real, must have
only a leaning, begged, and permitted nature—altogether false and contradictory. Divinity must be
complete and clear (out of idea), and therefore nothing.
Or, in being, it is at once as the " glass," and not the
" thing showing in the glass," and as divinity is only

possible under idea of it, which is not the thing but the *idea* of the thing, and as the idea of the thing is the only thing possible (if we are not ourselves God), there is nothing other than the show, and no divinity at all. The world being it or God, or the human reason. Thus the human *reason* infallibly, under all its various heavenly deceits and just the more successfully according to its perfection, leads FROM God, and the idea of God (which is not God) is the very opposite of God, and being the very opposite of God, it must be the Evil-Principle. Nothingness is the non-holding of idea; of comparison, defect, or the devil—exempt and blank of meaning. Nothingness, as containing nothing; first "all," knowing no devil of "second" to find itself "first," and therefore (in the fact of being) conquered by the devil to discover itself, or be, at all. The reader will perceive that we are arguing for the Holy Spirit.

All this will only go to prove that, in the mere *human* reason, or *idea*, God is annihilated, and that he is only ultimately and really possible in the divine immediate possession, or in the supernatural *trampling* on Idea, and (to the world) madness or ecstacy. We can never rise to Him. He must descend to us. We can never make God. He must make us. He is only possible in thus snatching us out of the world, or out of ourselves. Michael-like, trampling us, and extinguishing us (Satan-like) first utterly out of idea. Which is the world, in which if we search for Him we shall fail to find. Otherwise, in miracle. Which miracles are disbelieved of the world, to be the very truest, and, in its disbelief, to be *made* true. That only true, being that not apparent. The faces of martyrs and saints, and the visible glory shining in them, as being not of the world, are the best proof—even to flesh—of God! Nothing of this miracle can be, else, got out of the things of the world. Nothing more distinct than in the transfiguration of the Holy, that, in miracle, have been illuminated out of flesh. And this is the cause, and the reason, of sainthood, and the why of its worship. It being substantially, and in verity, God.

And the disbelief and denial of Sainthood is the proof not only that it is true, but that the world—including human reason—is of evil, and is the devil; and, in denying it, the very thing not true—that being the only truth, and the other show only, to "cause existence," which is true only in the belief of it. That is, as man is.

As the subtle spirit of the under-lying, and behind all nature, ambushed Fire, can throw all the chains of the great world loose, and spin the solid matter (in its waving wheels of the furnace), until it evaporates and delivers it up, expanded free, out of the touch of sense, so as at last not even unweighable gases, or clouds, or colours, into the great void; so, into this great, all-swallowing, fiercely unappeasable, utterly bottomless abyss of the resolving, melting, sundering, and evaporating splendour of metaphysic or Buddhist nothing-ness, can be cast all mind and all the delicate piecework of mind, all the qualities, all the affections, all the good, all the bad, all law, all form. In short, "all better and best," and the very power of thinking, as all the utterest consistency, or thought, worlds, or reason, or anything.

This is the end of this publication.

Any remaining blank pages are for our book binding
requirements and are blank on purpose.

To search thousands of interesting publications like this one,
please remember to visit our website at:

http://www.kessinger.net

Printed in the United Kingdom
by Lightning Source UK Ltd.
120761UK00001B/52